Would You Rather?

EASTER EDITION

By Uncle Bob

Illustrations by Steve Harlan
Cover designed by Angie Gerard

CONTENTS

III

RULES OF THE GAME

The rules are very basic.

- First of all, you need at least two players and you have to decide who is 'Player A' and 'Player B.' If you have a large group, you can even play with teams..

- Sit across from each other and make eye contact.

- We have 5 rounds and starting with 'Player A', read the question aloud and pick an answer. The same player will then explain why he/she chose that answer in the most hilarious way possible. Don't forget to use your silliest faces to get your opponent to crack a smile.

- If the reason makes 'Player B' laugh or even crack a smile, then 'Player A' gets a point.

- Take turns going back and forth, then mark your total laugh scores at the end of each round.

- Whoever gets the highest laugh score is officially crowned the 'Lord of the Laughs'!

REMEMBER, IF YOU ARE LAUGHING, YOU ARE LOSING!

Let's Get Cracking!

ROUND 1

1

"Funny & Silly Questions!"

WOULD YOU RATHER...

Have long bunny ears
dragging on the floor

~OR~

Long bunny feet that can't
fit in your shoes?

Spend the whole month dressed
as an Easter bunny

~OR~

Dressed as a giant chicken?

Laugh Score ⎨___/2

4

WOULD YOU RATHER...

Have a plastic
egg for your head

~OR~

Chocolate eyebrows?

Start each sentence with
"cock-a-doodle-doo"

~OR~

End each
sentence with "baa"?

Laugh Score ___/2

5

WOULD YOU RATHER...

Wear an Easter basket

-OR-

An eggshell as a hat to school?

Not be able
to stop jumping

-OR-

Not be able to stop
flapping your arms?

Laugh Score ____ /2

6

WOULD YOU RATHER...

Sneeze all Easter long

-OR-

Have uncontrollable farting during Easter dinner?

Have to paint
a thousand Easter eggs

-OR-

Decorate a thousand
Easter cookies?

Laugh Score ____/2

WOULD YOU RATHER...

**Do the bunny hop dance
in front of your class**

~OR~

**The chicken dance
in front of your crush?**

**Fly to the moon in
a carrot rocket**

~OR~

**Travel the world
in an egg car?**

Laugh Score ____/2

WOULD YOU RATHER...

Have a broken
egg on your head

~OR~

A "Happy Easter" tattoo all
over your forehead?

Have Easter grass
instead of your hair

~OR~

Lilies growing
out of your ears?

Laugh Score ⬭ /2

WOULD YOU RATHER...

Sleep in a bird's nest with
ten crying little birds

~OR~

In an Easter basket with ten
crying little chickens?

Have a fluffy bunny's tail
instead of your nose

~OR~

A beak instead of
your belly button?

Laugh Score [___/2]

WOULD YOU RATHER...

Always rush somewhere like the white rabbit from alice

-OR-

Start every conversation with "what's up, doc?" like bugs bunny?

Have your bum gain so much weight that it can't fit in a chair

-OR-

Have your belly gain so much weight that it is always sticking out under your shirt?

Laugh Score ____/2

WOULD YOU RATHER...

Have a puppy dressed
in a bunny costume

~OR~

A bunny dressed
in a chicken costume?

Say "Happy Easter" every
ten minutes for the whole week

~OR~

Sing an Easter song before every
meal for the whole month?

Laugh Score ____/2

WOULD YOU RATHER...

Have an angry bird
piloting your plane

-OR-

The march hare
driving your bus?

Be covered
in lamb's wool

-OR-

Chicken feathers?

Laugh Score ___ /2

Add up your points
and record them below!

Player _____ **/ 20**
ROUND TOTAL

Player _____ **/ 20**
ROUND TOTAL

Round 1
Winner _____

ROUND
2

"Weird Questions!"

WOULD YOU RATHER...

Be chased by a giant carrot with a tongue dragging on the ground

~OR~

By an Easter tree dressed as a princess?

Eat an Easter egg and get yellow spots all over your face

~OR~

Eat a carrot and get orange hair all over your body?

Laugh Score ____/2

WOULD YOU RATHER...

Pop an egg out of your mouth
whenever you cough

~OR~

Pop peeps out of your nose
whenever you sneeze?

Have the power to turn all rabbits
into chocolate bunnies

~OR~

To turn all chickens
into peeps?

Laugh Score ___/2

WOULD YOU RATHER...

Have all the
Easter-themed clothing

~OR~

All the rainbow-colored shoes?

Have an Easter basket that produces
5 chocolate eggs every ten minutes

~OR~

An Easter basket that produces one
giant chocolate egg every morning?

Laugh Score /2

WOULD YOU RATHER...

Look for one Easter egg hidden
in the sand on a long beach

-OR-

One Easter egg hidden in the snow
on the highest mountain?

Walk around covered
in thousands of confetti

-OR-

Covered in plastic
Easter grass?

Laugh Score ___/2

WOULD YOU RATHER...

Kiss a bunny and turn him
into a stinking monster

~OR~

Kiss a chicken and turn him
into a farting alien?

Have an egg fight
with your teacher

~OR~

A jelly bean fight
with your mother?

Laugh Score _____/2

20

WOULD YOU RATHER...

**Be a chicken without
a beak and wings**

~OR~

**A bunny without
a tail and ears?**

**Play "an Easter egg hunt" every night
for the rest of your life**

~OR~

**"Egg and spoon race" every morning
for the rest of your life?**

Laugh Score ____ /2

WOULD YOU RATHER...

Have marshmallows
fall instead of snow

~OR~

Hot chocolate
instead of rain?

Be a super bunny whose power is
to fire boogers from his ears

~OR~

A super chicken whose power is
to fire rolling eggs?

Laugh Score ____/2

WOULD YOU RATHER...

Turn into a panda when you eat a chocolate egg

~OR~

Turn into a sloth when you eat a rainbow pancake?

Live on a yacht surrounded by thousands of bleating lambs

~OR~

Be awakened every morning at 6 a.m. by a rooster in the mansion?

Laugh Score ____/2

WOULD YOU RATHER...

Celebrate Easter alone in
a house full of sweets

-OR-

With all your family and friends
without a single candy?

Be followed by a giant egg that
mimics your every move

-OR-

A giant egg that teases
you all day long?

Laugh Score ____ /2

24

WOULD YOU RATHER...

Have a three-eyed bunny

-OR-

A two-headed
chick for your pet?

Have to wear a pink
bunny ears headband

-OR-

Chicken legs shaped boots
wherever you go?

Laugh Score ⎯⎯/2

25

Add up your points
and record them below!

Player _____ **/ 20**

ROUND TOTAL

Player _____ **/ 20**

ROUND TOTAL

Round 2

Winner _____

ROUND

3

"Family
Questions!"

WOULD YOU RATHER...

Be raised in a burrow
by a rabbit family

~OR~

In a chicken coop by
a chicken family?

Have your family members with
chicken crests instead of their hair

~OR~

Family members with wings
instead of their ears?

Laugh Score ____/2

WOULD YOU RATHER...

Spend Easter with ten annoying sisters

~OR~

With ten crying baby brothers?

Let your mom dress you for Easter dinner

~OR~

Wear your grandma's Easter-themed sweater?

Laugh Score [__/2]

29

WOULD YOU RATHER...

Be the only chicken in your human family

~OR~

The only human in your chicken family?

Spend easter listening to your aunt's boring stories

~OR~

Talking to your bad-hearing grandfather?

Laugh Score ___/2

WOULD YOU RATHER...

Have an Easter photo with your family all dressed the same

-OR-

With your family all wearing bunny ears?

Be able to mute your mom's voice for Easter day

-OR-

To silence your dad's snoring for Easter night?

Laugh Score ____/2

31

WOULD YOU RATHER...

Be able to read minds to know where your family hid Easter eggs

-OR-

Have super speed to find all the Easter eggs first?

Have your mom pick you up from school wearing an Easter basket as her hat

-OR-

Have your dad bring you to a school dance dressed as a chicken?

Laugh Score _____/2

WOULD YOU RATHER...

Turn your brother's head into marshmallow peeps

-OR-

Your sister's legs into chicken drumsticks?

Get $5 from your granny for easter to spend as you wish

-OR-

A $1000 that you can't spend until you are eighteen?

Laugh Score ____/2

WOULD YOU RATHER...

Have a grandma who thinks she is a chicken and flaps her arms

~OR~

A grandpa who thinks he is a dog and barks at sheep?

Have a sister as funny as babs bunny

~OR~

A brother as smart as eggbert?

Laugh Score ___/2

WOULD YOU RATHER...

Become your mom and make
a whole Easter feast

~OR~

Become your dad and clean the
whole house for the Easter holidays?

Have your family Easter dinner at the
top of the empire state building

~OR~

In the middle of the
golden gate bridge?

Laugh Score ⬡___/2

WOULD YOU RATHER...

Have a super
strong captain carrot

~OR~

A clumsy but funny foghom
leghom for your dad?

Let your sister pull your
nose whenever you want to
get a chocolate egg

~OR~

Let your brother pull your
ears whenever you want to get
jelly beans?

Laugh Score ____/2

WOULD YOU RATHER...

Be the president's child and have an Easter party at the white house

-OR-

The queen's child and have an Easter party at court?

Wake up on Easter and find out that your family speaks the klingon language

-OR-

That your family doesn't speak at all?

Laugh Score ⬡ /2

Add up your points and record them below!

Player ____ **/ 20**
ROUND TOTAL

Player ____ **/ 20**
ROUND TOTAL

Round 3 Winner _____

ROUND
4

"Gross Questions!"

WOULD YOU RATHER...

Get a rash whenever you
eat a chocolate egg

~OR~

Get uncontrollable itching
whenever you eat peeps?

Find an Easter egg in
a dirty trash bin

~OR~

In your grandpa's
stinking sock?

Laugh Score _____ /2

WOULD YOU RATHER...

Eat jelly beans that taste like moldy cauliflower

~OR~

Peeps that taste like raw eggs?

Get an Easter basket full of frogs

~OR~

See worms on your Easter egg tree?

Laugh Score ___/2

41

WOULD YOU RATHER...

Burp Butterflies

-OR-

Fart glitter all Easter long?

Always have brown stuff under your nails

-OR-

Have your hair smeared with egg yolk?

Laugh Score [___/2]

WOULD YOU RATHER...

Eat a ten-year-old chocolate egg

-OR-

An unbaked Easter cookie?

Come to school smelling
like a modly egg

-OR-

Like stinky cheese?

Laugh Score ____ /2

WOULD YOU RATHER...

Find out that your mom made an Easter cake with her feet

~OR~

That your grandma chewed and spat on all your jelly beans?

Eat a chocolate egg you found in the toilet

~OR~

Drink some Easter punch from your boot?

Laugh Score ____/2

44

WOULD YOU RATHER...

Go to school with Easter grass
stuck in your nose

~OR~

With jelly beans
stuck in your teeth?

find your grandpa's toenail
in a chocolate egg

~OR~

Your grandma's nose hair
in pancakes?

Laugh Score ___/2

WOULD YOU RATHER...

Have to lick your friend's armpit to get an Easter egg

-OR-

Let your friend lick your armpit to get an Easter egg from you?

Step on a bunny's poop

-OR-

Smell a lamb's bum?

Laugh Score ____/2

WOULD YOU RATHER...

Eat an Easter egg and get
a hairy tongue

~OR~

Eat a lilly's petal and get
a stinky belly button?

Wake up for Easter next
to baby's puke

~OR~

Change a baby's diaper
all Easter long?

Laugh Score ____/2

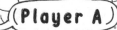

WOULD YOU RATHER...

Have bad gas during your
family Easter dinner

~OR~

Diarrhea in front
of your class?

Brush your teeth
with egg yolk

~OR~

Wash your face
with vinegar?

Laugh Score _____/2

48

WOULD YOU RATHER...

Turn into a giant chicken
covered in yucky warts

~OR~

Into a bunny covered in
stinky pimples?

Have a fart that smells like rotten
eggs in front of your class

~OR~

A burp that smells like
an onion in front of your crush?

Laugh Score ___/2

Add up your points and record them below!

Player _____ **/ 20**
ROUND TOTAL

Player _____ **/ 20**
ROUND TOTAL

Round 4 Winner _____

ROUND
5

"Food & Drink
Questions!"

WOULD YOU RATHER...

Take a bath in a tub filled
with chocolate

~OR~

Swim in the pool filled
with jelly beans?

Have to eat
20 carrots for dinner

~OR~

Drink 5 egg yolks for breakfast?

Laugh Score ___/2

WOULD YOU RATHER...

Pour pepper
into the Easter punch

~OR~

Pour salt into an Easter
chocolate cake?

Be able to eat only Easter candies
for the rest of your life

~OR~

Never be able to
eat jelly beans again?

Laugh Score ____/2

53

WOULD YOU RATHER...

Bite a fake wooden egg

-OR-

Be smashed with a raw egg?

Swallow all the peeps
without chewing

-OR-

Always have marshmallows
glued to your teeth?

Laugh Score ⌐____/2

54

WOULD YOU RATHER...

Live in a house
with jelly furniture

-OR-

In a house
with egg floors?

Turn your mom's
hands into carrots

-OR-

Your dad's belly
into an egg?

Laugh Score ____ /2

WOULD YOU RATHER...

Find a cockroach in a chocolate egg

~OR~

A worm in your Easter biscuit?

Eat onion flavored jelly beans

~OR~

Mushroom flavored peeps?

Laugh Score ___/2

WOULD YOU RATHER...

find out that there is no candy
in your Easter basket

-OR-

That there is no money in
your Easter egg?

Not be able to drink water
after eating a chocolate

-OR-

Have to drink lemonade every
10 minutes throughout Easter?

Laugh Score [____/2

57

Player A

WOULD YOU RATHER...

Eat soup
made of frogs

~OR~

Juice made of owl eyes
for Easter lunch?

Eat all Easter eggs
with ketchup

~OR~

All jelly beans
with mayonnaise?

Laugh Score ⌐__/2

58

WOULD YOU RATHER...

Have your family eat Easter
dinner with their feet

-OR-

Have your family go naked
on an "egg hunt"?

Drink nettle juice and get
a swollen tongue on Easter

-OR-

Drink soda and start to pop out
bubbles through your nose for the
rest of your life?

Laugh Score ____/2

WOULD YOU RATHER...

**Eat spaghetti
through your nose**

~OR~

**Peeps through
your ears?**

**Have marshmallow–
shaped fingertips**

~OR~

Chocolate flavored nails?

Laugh Score ___/2

60

WOULD YOU RATHER...

Have all the Easter sweets
that are salty

-OR-

The chicken drumsticks
that are sweet?

Have pickles and peanut butter
for Easter breakfast

-OR-

Pancakes with chili and
nutella for Easter dinner?

Laugh Score ____/2

61

Add up your points
and record them below!

Player _____ **/ 20**
ROUND TOTAL

Player _____ **/ 20**
ROUND TOTAL

Round 5
Winner

_____

EASTER JOKES

"Egg-cellent Jokes to Crack You Up!"

How can
you send a letter
to the Easter Bunny?

By hare mail.

Why you
shouldn't tell an
Easter egg
a good joke?

Because it might
crack up!

What do you call a very tired Easter egg?

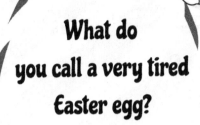

Eggs–austed.

How do you know the Bunny is really smart?

Because he's an egghead.

Where does the Bunny get his eggs?

From Eggplants.

What happened to the rabbit when he misbehaved at school?

He was eggspelled!

What is
the rabbit's
favorite kind
of music?

Hip-hop,
of course!

How did
the Easter Bunny
dry himself?

With a
hare dryer!

How do
Easter Bunnies
stay cool during
the summer?

With hare
conditioning.

How does
the Easter Bunny
travel?

By hare-plane.

**What day
of the week do
Easter eggs hate
the most?**

fry-days!

**What do
you call
a deaf donkey?**

Anything you like,
he can't hear you!

What kind of jewelry does the Bunny wear?

14 Carrot gold.

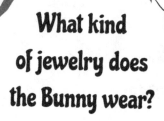

How do you know the Easter Bunny liked his vacation?

Because he said it was egg-cellent!

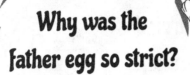

Why was the father egg so strict?

He was hard-boiled.

What two animals have the same last name?

The donKEY and the monKEY.

**What happens
if you get married
on Easter Sunday?**

You live
hoppily ever after.

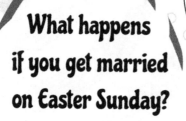

**How does the
Bunny stay in shape?**

He does lots
of eggs–ercises.

How does Easter end?

With the letter 'R'.

What came first, the chick or the egg?

Neither, it's the Easter Bunny.

Why don't you see dinosaurs at Easter time?

Because they're eggs-tinct.

Why do eggs go to school?

To get egg-ducated!

What kind of stories do Easter Bunnies like best?

Ones with hoppy endings.

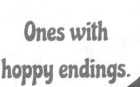

Why did the bunny cross the road?

No bunny knows.

Why did the cow
to Hollywood?

Because she wanted
to be a movie star.

What do
you call an
Easter Bunny
with the sniffles?

A runny bunny!

Knock, knock.
Who's there?
Esther.
Esther who?
Esther Bunny!

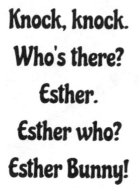

Knock, Knock.
Who's there?
Bing.
Bing who?
Bing me some
candy please
Mr. Easter bunny.

78

Knock, Knock.
Who's there?
Carrie.
Carrie who?
Carrie my
Easter basket please,
it's too heavy.

Knock, Knock.
Who's there?
Hans.
Hans who?
Hans off my
Easter candy buster!

Knock, Knock.
Who's there?
Happy.
Happy who?
Happy Easter!

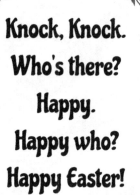

Knock, knock.
Who's there?
Ann.
Ann who?
Ann Easter bunny
(An Easter bunny)

Knock, knock.
Who's there?
No more.
No more who?
No more Easter bunnies,
wait till next year!

Knock, Knock.
Who's there?
Holly.
Holly who?
Hollyulujah – it's Easter.

Knock, knock.
Who's there?
Dozen.
Dozen who?
Dozen anyone
find eggs yet.

Knock, knock.
Who's there?
Says.
Says who?
Says me!

Knock, Knock.
Who's there?
Some bunny.
Some bunny who?
Some bunny is eating
all my Easter eggs!

Knock, Knock.
Who's there?
Eggs.
Eggs who?
Eggs–cited for
the Easter Bunny!

Knock, knock.
Who's there?
Justin.
Justin who?
Justin time to
do the Bunny Hop!

Knock, knock.
Who's there?
Donut.
Donut who?
Donut forget to
say Happy Easter!

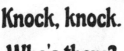

Knock, knock.
Who's there?
Police.
Police who?
Police hurry up and
decorate your eggs.

Knock, knock.
Who's there?
Hawaii.
Hawaii who?
I'm fine, Hawaii you?

Knock, knock.
Who's there?
Freddie.
Freddie who?
Freddie for Easter.

Knock, knock.
Who's there?
Boo.
Boo who?
Don't cry – all the
Easter bunnies
will be back again
next year!

86

"EASTER MAZE"

Help the pencils find the way out of the middle of the maze and paint all four eggs!

CONCLUSION

Congratulations! You're truly amazing! I am sure there are some obstacles along the way; it was great you persisted through and finished the job!

If you want to continue with some more funny 'would you rather questions', just send me an email to notanaverage23@gmail.com and I will send you some printable questions for free.

My name is Robert Ellis, a.k.a Uncle Bob and I'd like to say "thank you" for purchasing my book and I hope that you had as much fun reading it as I had writing it.

If you have any suggestions about how to improve this book, changes to make or how to make it more useful, please let me know.

If you like this book, would you be so kind and leave a review on Amazon.

I bid you farewell and wishing you and your family a lot of love and happiness!

Thank you very much and good luck! ☺

— Uncle Bob

Would You Rather Book for Kids - Crazy & Gross Edition: The Ultimate Collection of "Would You Rather" Questions for Kids 6-12 Years Old (Game Book with Silly Illustrations)

Would You Rather? EWW! Edition:
The Funniest Collection of "Would You Rather"
Questions for Kids 6-12 Years Old (Game Book
for Kids with Silly Illustrations)

ABOUT THE AUTHOR

Robert Ellis, a.k.a Uncle Bob, is the eldest child and only son with three younger sisters of a former school teacher and nurse mother from Boston, Massachusetts. He wasn't always the funniest or smartest kid at school... but one fateful day everything changed for him.

When Uncle Bob was a 10-year-old boy, he received a very old and a super rare book of jokes as a birthday gift from his grandma. It was definitely the best present in his life. Since then, his dream to become a children's book author and to write the most hilarious jokes became an obsession.

Uncle Bob is also a dad of two funny goofy kids and husband of a beautiful wife.

In his spare time, Uncle Bob loves to hike, fish, visit the beach, and do anything remotely adventurous, like zip-lining.

As an author, he hopes to inspire children to have a love of learning and a passion for reading. He is excited to share his work with you!

Hopefully, his books will make people all around the world a little bit kinder, healthier, and happier!